Violin Exam Pieces

ABRSM Grade 1

Selected from the 2012–2015 syllabus

Name

Date of exam

GW01048805

Contents

Violin consultant: Philippa Bunting
Footnotes: Edward Huws Jones (EHJ) and Anthony Burton

Other pieces for Grade 1

LIST A

4 **Anon. 17th-century English** The Duke of Lorraine's March. *Violin Star 2*, arr. Huws Jones (ABRSM)

5 **T. Arne** Allegro (from *The Fairy Prince*). No. 32 from *Violin Playtime*, Book 2, arr. de Keyser (Faber)

6 **Purcell** Rondeau. P. 47 from *Superstart Violin (The Complete Method)*, arr. Cohen (Faber)

LIST B

4 **Kathy and David Blackwell** The Old Castle. No. 39 from *Fiddle Time Joggers*, arr. Blackwell (OUP)

5 **Holst** Jupiter Theme (from *The Planets*). *Classical Pieces for Violin*, arr. van Rompaey (De Haske)

6 **Sullivan** The Merryman and his Maid. *Piece by Piece 2 for Violin*, arr. Nelson (Boosey & Hawkes)

LIST C

4 **Peter Martin** Hoe Down: from *Little Suite No. 3* (Stainer & Bell)

5 **Sheila Nelson** Fiddler's Fancy: No. 19 from *Right from the Start – Violin* (Boosey & Hawkes)

6 **Trad. Greek** Arcadian Dance (violin melody) (lower line only in *col legno*; open E string on final note). *The Greek Fiddler*, arr. Huws Jones (Boosey & Hawkes)

First published in 2011 by ABRSM (Publishing) Ltd, a wholly owned subsidiary of ABRSM, 24 Portland Place, London W1B 1LU, United Kingdom © 2011 by The Associated Board of the Royal Schools of Music

Music origination by Andrew Jones
Cover by Økvik Design
Printed in England by Halstan & Co. Ltd, Amersham, Bucks

MIX
Paper from responsible sources
FSC™ C109619

Mattachins

Arranged by Edward Huws Jones

Thoinot Arbeau

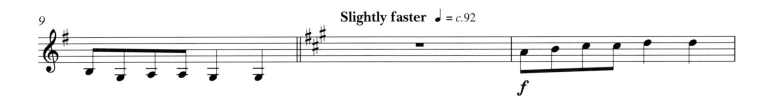

A 'mattachins' is a sword dance that was popular in Europe from the 16th century to the 18th. The tune included here first appeared in print in Arbeau's *Orchésographie* (1588), alongside pictures showing how the dance should be performed. The tune was given a new lease of life when Peter Warlock included it in his *Capriol Suite* (1926). The sword-dancing origins suggest how it should be played: it needs to be lively and boisterous! EHJ

Menuet

from *Music for the Royal Fireworks*, HWV 351

A:2

Arranged by Lionel Salter

G. F. Handel

George Frideric Handel (1685–1759) was born in Germany, but spent the last 47 years of his life in England, where he became famous as a composer of operas, oratorios and instrumental music. In 1749, he wrote his *Music for the Royal Fireworks* to accompany a fireworks display in Green Park in London celebrating the end of a European war. It was played by a band of about 100 musicians: oboes, bassoons, horns, trumpets and drums, and probably strings as well, in defiance of King George II's reported remark that 'he hoped there would be no fiddles'. The music consists of a large-scale overture followed by a series of dance movements, of which this joyful minuet is the last.

A:3

German Dance

from K. 605 No. 3

Arranged by Mary Cohen

W. A. Mozart

The Austrian composer Wolfgang Amadeus Mozart (1756–91) wrote operas, symphonies, concertos and many other major works, but also numerous sets of dances – many of them, in the later part of his life, in fulfilment of his duties as 'chamber musician' to the Austro-Hungarian Emperor at the court in Vienna. This German Dance (a forerunner of the waltz) comes from a set of three for orchestra which Mozart wrote in February 1791 for a carnival dance in Vienna. Its middle section or trio, not included in this arrangement, is the well-known *Die Schlittenfahrt* (Sleigh Ride) with five jingling sleigh bells.

Sandmännchen

No. 4 from *Volks-Kinderlieder*, WoO 31

B:1

Arranged by Lionel Salter

Johannes Brahms

Sandmännchen Little Sandman; **Volks-Kinderlieder** Folksongs for Children

The German composer Johannes Brahms (1833–97), famous for his symphonies and concertos, had a strong interest in folk music, and published several collections of arrangements of German folksongs. The first of these, which appeared in 1858, was a set of *Volks-Kinderlieder*, dedicated to the young children of his mentors Robert and Clara Schumann. It includes 'Sandmännchen', a song about the mythical Sandman who lulls children to sleep and brings them pleasant dreams by sprinkling magic sand into their eyes. This arrangement preserves not only the melody of the song but also Brahms's piano part, although it shortens the original postlude.

B:2

The Boat to Inverie

Edward Huws Jones

The Scottish village of Inverie is one of the most isolated communities on the British mainland. The only access to it is by boat or a 20-mile walk across the hills. EHJ

Edward Huws Jones (born 1948) is a well-known composer and arranger, with a wide-ranging knowledge of fiddle playing styles around the world and a special interest in music for young string players. He has acted as consultant and editor for ABRSM on numerous projects. *The Boat to Inverie*, in the style of a Scottish folksong, is from his *Violin Star* series.

© 2011 by The Associated Board of the Royal Schools of Music
Reproduced from Huws Jones: *Violin Star 2* (ABRSM)

Daisy Bell

B:3

Arranged by Mark Mumford

Harry Dacre

The English songwriter Harry Dacre (1860–1922) had his biggest hit in 1892 with his waltz-time song *Daisy Bell*, a favourite in the music halls of both London and New York. It remained popular for many years, and in 1961 became the first song ever sung by a computer. This arrangement presents just the chorus, to the words:

> Daisy, Daisy, give me your answer, do,
> I'm half crazy all for the love of you.
> It won't be a stylish marriage –
> I can't afford a carriage,
> But you'll look sweet, on the seat
> Of a bicycle built for two.

Pennsylvania 6-5000

Jerry Gray
and Carl Sigman

Jerry Gray (1915–76) was an American composer and arranger of the big band era, well known for his work with the bandleaders Artie Shaw and Glenn Miller. It was for the Glenn Miller Orchestra in 1940 that Gray, in collaboration with Carl Sigman (1909–2000), wrote *Pennsylvania 6-5000* – named after the telephone number of the Hotel Pennsylvania in New York, where the Orchestra was appearing at the Café Rouge Ballroom. This arrangement comes from the collection *What Jazz 'n' Blues Can I Play?*, edited by Mark Mumford and Tim Siddall. The editors suggest unhurried swung quavers (as indicated above), slightly shortened crotchets in bar 2 and similar bars and 'some crescendo for expressive effect within phrases'.

Russia – Gopak

No. 5 from *Travel Tunes*

C:2

Margery Dawe

'Margery Dawe' – the pseudonym (writing name) of a music teacher in south-east London, who died in 2001 – composed and arranged many books of educational music for piano, recorder and various string instruments. This piece comes from a collection of six *Travel Tunes* for violin or viola or cello and piano, published in the 1950s. It is in the style of the gopak (or hopak), the energetic national dance of Ukraine, which is now an independent country but was formerly part of the Russian Empire and then the Soviet Union.

C:3

Dvoják

Couple Dance

Arranged by Leoš Faltus

Leoš Janáček

Leoš Janáček (1854–1928) was born in a village in Moravia, in the eastern part of the present-day Czech Republic, and lived for many years in the Moravian capital, Brno. He was an enthusiastic collector of the folksongs and dances of his native region, which influenced the melodies and rhythms of his operas and other music, and which he also published in his own arrangements. This is a version for violin and piano of Janáček's sketch for a piano arrangement of a couple dance from the Haná region, in alternating pairs of bars of 2/4 and 3/4 with the crotchet beat constant.

05/13